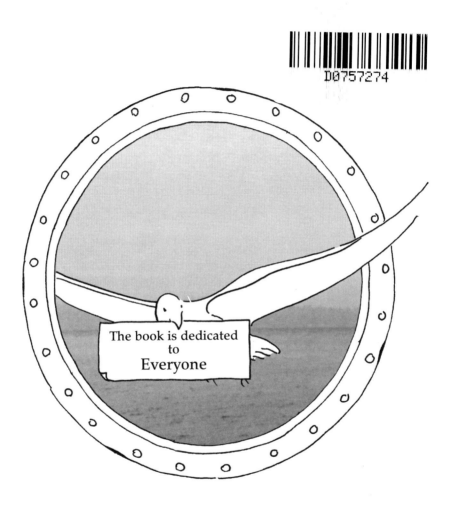

The book is dedicated
to
Everyone

Published by Inner Eye Publishing
P.O. Box 559
Mt. Shasta, CA, 96067

Copyeditor: Margot Silk Forrest
Design: Nancy Marie
Mechanicals: Marie-Josée Studio, Mt. Shasta, CA
Cover Design: Nancy Marie

Marie, Nancy 1947–
    Passage of Change : A fable based on the research of
Bruce Lipton, Ph.D. / written and illustrated by Nancy Marie.
    p. cm.
    LCCN 2003108226
    ISBN 0-9660418-2-8

    1. Lipton, Bruce—Fiction. 2. Mins and Body—Fiction.
3. Cell interaction—Fiction. 4. Psychophysiology—Fiction.
5. Perception—Fiction. I. Title.

PS3613.A744P37 2003   813'.6
                             QBI33-1571

Publisher will plant two trees
for every tree used to produce
this book.

Printed on acid-free recycled paper with soy-based ink.

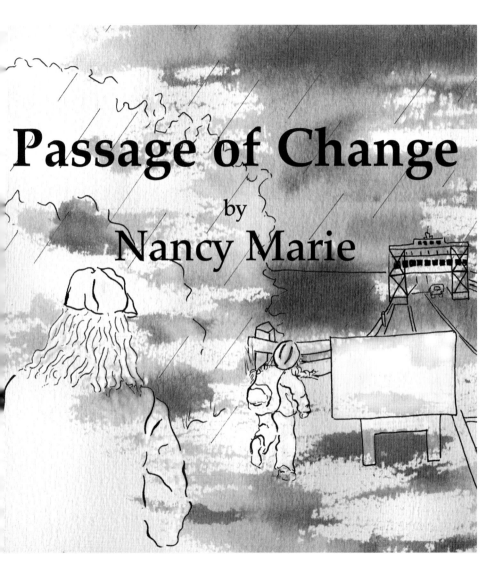

Passage of Change

by

Nancy Marie

Foreword

Earlier in my career as a research scientist and medical school professor, I actively supported the perspective that the human body was "biochemical machine 'programmed' by its genes." We scientists believe that human strengths, such as artistic or intellectual abilities, and weaknesses, such as cardiovascular disease, cancer or depression, were traits that had been preprogrammed into our genes. Hence, I perceived life attributes and deficits, as well as our health and our frailties, as merely reflection of our heredity.

In 1980, however, my research began to reveal that this perspective on the nature of life was flawed. By 1985 I realized that rather than being controlled by our genes, our cells are controlled by their perception of the environment. I formulated a hypothesis that the "brain" of the cell was actually the cell membrane, and I was offered an opportunity to test this hypothesis as a research fellow at Stanford University's School of Medicine in 1987. My theory on the control of our cells by our perceptions was substantiated in two major scientific publications. This pioneering research presaged one of today's most active areas of investigation, epigenetics, the science of how genes are controlled by the environment and—more importantly—by our perception of that environment.

This new perspective on human biology does not view the body as just a mechanical device, but incorporates the role of mind and spirit. This breakthrough in the science of biology is fundamental to healing, for it shows us that when we change our perceptions or beliefs we send totally different messages to our cells. In effect, we reprogram them. This new biology reveals why people can have spontaneous remissions or recover from injuries thought to be permanent disabilities.

The body really represents the cooperative effort of a community of fifty trillion single cells. While every cell is an independent entity, the body's community accommodates the wishes and intents of its "central voice"—the mind and spirit.

Our principle source of stress is our mind, which really consists of two separate "minds"—the conscious and the subconscious. The conscious mind is the thinking "you." It is the creative mind that expresses free will. Its supporting partner is the subconscious mind, a database of programmed behaviors. Some "programs" are derived from genetics. However, the vast majority of our subconscious programs are acquired through the developmental learning experiences we have as children.

The subconscious mind is not the seat of reasoning or creative consciousness. It is strictly a stimulus-response device. When the subconscious mind perceives a signal from its environment, it reflexively responds by activating a previously stored behavioral response—no thinking required!

Our fundamental perceptions or beliefs about life were downloaded into our subconscious mind as we simply observed the behaviors and attitudes of our parents, siblings and peers during the first six years of our lives. Our adult mind's effectiveness *now* is defined by the quality of the programs carried in our subconscious mind.

The insidious part is that our subconscious behaviors are programmed to engage without the control of, nor observation by, the conscious self. Since most of our behaviors are under the control of the subconscious mind, we rarely observe them, much less know that they are even engaged.

When we become more conscious and rely less on the automated programs in our subconscious, we become the masters of our fates rather than the "victims" of our programs. Using our conscious awareness we can actively transform our lives by rewriting our limiting perceptions and beliefs as well as our self-sabotaging behaviors.

Nancy Marie has presented this new scientific awareness in such a simple and whimsical manner that she engages the reader's whole brain, thus creating a pathway in support of new conscious awareness and change. Once that understanding is present you can begin to view life from a new perspective and actively change your old beliefs. As Nancy so eloquently puts it, "Now, beliefs don't just vanish with a single wish or prayer. You need to consciously remove those old beliefs in there...Change can happen quickly or it can take lots of time, but eventually your sense of self you will completely redefine."

Bruce Lipton, Ph.D.
Santa Cruz, California
July 15, 2003

Acknowledgments

It takes a community of hearts and minds to birth a book. I was blessed with such a fellowship throughout the creation of *Passage of Change*.

To begin with, I am grateful for Dr. Bruce Lipton's insights, his research and his desire to get this information out to the general public.

I am grateful for my highly insightful editor, Margot Silk Forrest, for her ability to see a book's potential and for knowing how to get there.

I am thankful that my friends Nancy Bauer, Susan Elson, Anca Hariton, Ana Holub, Margaret Horton, Faye and Sechi Kimura, Karla Maree, Erik Olesen, and Mary Olson were willing to read the manuscript and give me constructive feedback in its many stages of development.

I am grateful for my artist friends Anca Hariton, Kim Solga, and Lisa Mallory for helping me develop the illustrations in a manner that both guided the reader and illuminated the text.

I am also grateful to my friend Catherine Keir who facilitated my trip to Seattle so I could get the images into my mind.

There were also numerous other individuals who supported and encouraged me with their enthusiasm throughout this project. I am grateful for every one of them.

Special thanks goes to my husband Alan, a wordsmith extraordinaire, who knew me before my words flowed so freely. It was his gift with words that has truly inspired me over the years to let my words carve images that delight my soul.

Finally special thanks goes to my amazing children, Molly and Caton. They always help me to remember who I am and why I am here.

Passage of Change

by

Nancy Marie

A fable based on the research of Bruce Lipton, Ph.D.

Clutching my ticket
in the chilling rain,
I boarded the ferry,
wrestling with my pain.

All I could think about
was retreating inside,
but the ferry was crowded,
the only seats were outside.

3

The whistle blew loud.
They hauled in the plank.
I pulled my coat closer
as my mood sank.

Why am I always so
frightened and scared,
unable to trust
and filled with despair?

I wish I could learn
to be clear and strong,
to trust in myself
and feel like I belong.

I had just settled down
in a solitary place,
when around the corner
a woman showed her face.

She was vibrant and alive,
greeting all on her way,
even talking to gulls,
as she enjoyed her day.

7

The rain turned to fog
as I hid from the crowd.
As the boat lunged forward,
she laughed out loud!

She opened her coat
and let the wind blow through;
she undid her hair
and kicked off her shoes.

"I love this weather,"
she began to sing.
*"It reminds me I'm alive
and part of everything."*

10

I huddled in my corner,
trying to ignore this scene,
for all of her happiness
made me want to scream.

"I used to be like you,"
she abruptly turned and said.
*"I was lost and wounded,
filled with fears and misled."*

Now the waves grew bigger
and the boat was rocking more.
I felt like shrinking,
but her joy continued to soar.

*"I know your life isn't working
the way you want it to,
and you have the same problems
no matter what you do."*

My mouth flew open,
my jaw fell down.
I sputtered and made
an unintelligible sound.

14

How could she know
what was going on in me?
How was that possible?
How could that be?

Then as if she had heard
the thoughts I just had,
she said, *"I know those feelings
that are making you so sad.*

"I repeated my troubles
and made the same mistakes.
I felt stupid and overwhelmed
by frequent heartbreak.

"I had asked for assistance
from everyone I knew.
Some said it was karma,
and there was nothing I could do.

16

*"I refused that sentence
for it felt like the end.
But I was still unhappy
and could no longer pretend."*

I sputtered some more
trying to get out a word,
but she kept on talking
and flapped her arms like a bird.

17

"Others said my problems
were caused by my genes:
'Genes are responsible
for all that's seen or unseen.'

"But that made me a victim
and unresponsible, too.
For if it was just my genes,
there was nothing I could do.

"Then I found the answer
I had sought my whole life long.
It's the key to my happiness
and helps me stay strong."

19

The fog began lifting.
The waters had calmed down.
And my spirits started rising
as we floated across the sound.

21

"I may seem different
and act crazy to you.
But I've studied this science,
and what I tell you is true.

"To really make a difference
and to make a change that's good,
the laws of science and nature
must be completely understood.

"They need to work together
like the crew on this boat.
So listen and I will teach you
how to keep your life afloat."

I just sat there and stared,
not knowing what to say.
This was really becoming
the most amazing day.

The woman began smiling,
her hair flew every which way,
and her eyes were sparkling
as these words she did say.

23

"You are made up of over
fifty **trillion** tiny cells,
all working together
to help you move, taste and smell.

"A cell's membrane
is just like your skin,
for it helps the cell see
what happens outside and within.

"It has little receptors
in its membrane wall
to observe environmental changes
from the large to the small."

24

I was getting irritated,
but she continued along.
"How can this help me change
the things that feel so wrong?"

*"Knowing this information
can help you understand
what is holding you back
and how to truly expand."*

The fog grew even lighter,
it was now barely a mist.
My mind was also opening—
her words were the catalyst.

*"Your cells are a community,
like a village or a tribe.
They work together to fulfill
any tasks your brain decides.*

*"Every cell in your body
is like a silicon chip.
Encoded in its nucleus
is your genetic script.*

*"Some think the nucleus
is the brain of the cell,
but it only stores blueprints
to help keep the cell well.*

"Its brain is its membrane,
while its receptors respond,
and with the environment
it does correspond.

"Only cells that are needed
will respond to a call.
They know it's their turn
when the signal passes through their wall.

"Now each cell is **reprogrammable**,
but not by your genes.
Its source of information is
your belief about what you've seen.

29

"Are you saying
that what I believe
can bend or distort
the way I perceive?"

*"If any of your beliefs
are inaccurate or untrue,
your perceptions can be slanted,
your whole life misconstrued."*

"This is important!"
I moved to where she stood.
"If what you say is true,
this truth must be understood."

"Our beliefs come from experiences
or what we **think** we see.
Gaining clarity about them
can really set us free."

"When does this all happen?
Where does it take place?
How can I find the beliefs
that make my life a rat race?"

"This whole process begins
while we are in the womb
because that's where Mother Nature
prepares us to grow and bloom."

"How could I form a belief
before I was even born?
How could I have an opinion
when I was barely a form?"

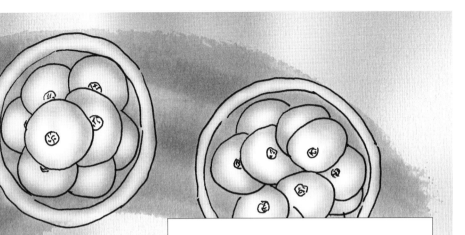

"Your mother's beliefs and perceptions
were chemically passed to you
by how she reacted
and what she thought was true.

"Your cells knew she was preparing
you to live your new life.
So it listened to her messages—
whether harmony or strife.

"That set up a pattern,
a way of approaching each day.
So unless you change the message
your life may go the same way."

I wanted to say something,
but I just stood there and stared.
I knew I had found the answer
to my ongoing despair.

"If you received the message:
Life is filled with harm,
your brain would sound
your protection alarm.

"Your cells would stop growth
so they could defend instead,
until a new message
was heard in your head.

*"But if the message said
life would be safe and good,
you could grow and evolve
like you really should."*

"The problems I am having
stem from messages I received?
And these messages influence
the way I **now** perceive?"

*"Your cells have but two choices,
either grow or defend.
On how you view your environment,
their action will depend."*

The sky was getting clearer
and so was my mind,
as the answers to my questions
I began to find.

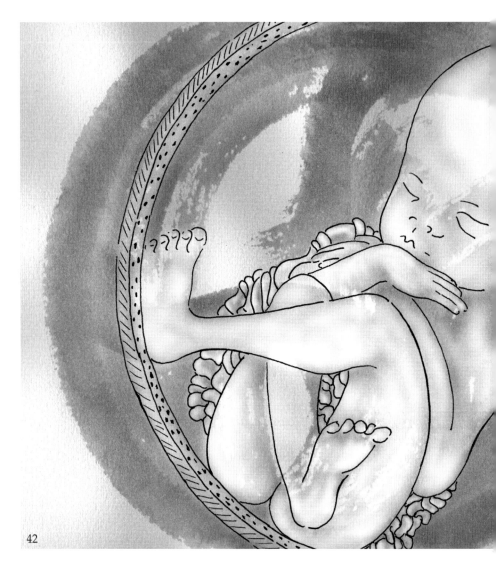

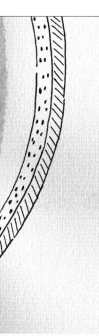

"When we grow in the womb
the choice is not our own.
Our bodies merely respond
to the impulse we are shown.

"Then we repeat the same behaviors
we learned when we were small
until we can change the belief
that caused our own downfall."

"So if I change my beliefs,
my perceptions will change too?
And my ongoing confusion
will discontinue?"

"If as a child your perceptions
became distorted or confected,
then self-sabotaging behavior
can certainly be expected.

"But when you become clear
and know what you want to do,
you can change those beliefs
and create a life that fits you."

43

"But what can I do?
Is there a way to know?
How can I change old beliefs
and allow myself to grow?"

*"If you find a problem
appearing time and again,
pay attention, this is where
your inner change can begin.*

*"Instead of viewing the problem
as something dreadfully wrong,
imagine it is showing you
what to change to grow strong.*

*"Then find the old beliefs
at the root of the mess
and replace them with new visions
with more hope and less stress."*

44

"Can it really be that easy?
That's all I have to do,
to correct the old beliefs
that are quite misconstrued?"

*"Now, beliefs don't just vanish
with a single wish or prayer.
You need to consciously remove
those old beliefs in there.*

*"For from your parents
these beliefs may have come,
but now your brain repeats them
until you change or succumb.*

*"Change can happen quickly
or it can take lots of time,
but eventually your sense of self
you will completely redefine."*

45

"Stay conscious in the moment,
don't hide in the future or past.
This will crystallize your clarity
and create a change that can last.

"Then get to know your spirit
and what your heart holds dear.
And get to know what beliefs rule you
when you aren't truly clear.

"For from this knowledge,
a new life you can grow
that reflects who you are
and what you really know."

The sun was coming out,
sea gulls were everywhere.
A new sense of freedom
was floating in the air.

49

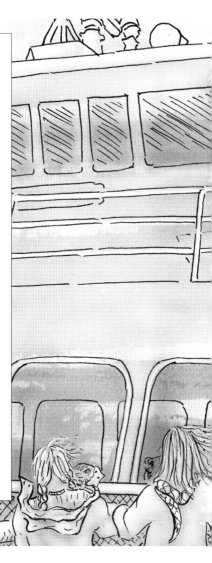

"Could I have gotten the message
that I shouldn't try to succeed?
And would that single message
my power and growth impede?"

"If when you were young,
you felt unsafe, wrong, or bad,
then you can easily end up feeling
disempowered or sad.

"But you can change those beliefs.
You can change how you perceive,
and that will affect your life
and what you receive.

"When a new problem arises
you won't have to run or hide.
Instead new wisdom and growth
you can let it provide.

"Now you'll know you've succeeded
in deleting crippling beliefs
by how you react to obstacles
and your newfound sense of relief."

"So even if I got the message
of being unworthy, wrong, or bad,
I don't have to recreate
the problems my ancestors had?

"By changing my old beliefs
I can see a different way,
and this will affect
everything I think, do, or say?"

Then she smiled at me
in such a caring way,
I knew I had understood
the things she told me today.

"Is there anything else
I need to know
to stop the confusion
and help myself to grow?"

52

"Just remember when you're stressed,
growth is always deferred,
and when that happens,
disease or imbalance can occur.

"That creates more anxiety
from which you have to defend,
which means you lose your ability
to grow, trust, and mend.

"But reprogramming can continue
throughout your whole life,
for whenever you are conscious,
you can change beliefs and reduce strife.

"Now, it all works quite simply
and is easy to comprehend,
but only if your brain's message
is clearly what you intend."

The whistle blew,
signaling the end of the line,
but my heart knew that forever more
my life could be just fine.

The plank went down,
the crowd walked onto the pier.
I turned to thank my friend
but she had disappeared.

Yet I left the boat knowing
this journey had helped me see
how my old beliefs were holding me back
and how changing them would set me free.

The End

Bruce H. Lipton, Ph.D., cellular biologist and author, was formerly an Associate Professor of Anatomy at the University of Wisconsin's School of Medicine (1973-1982), where he taught medical students and researched muscular dystrophy. As a Fellow in Pathology at Stanford University's School of Medicine (1987–1992), his published research on cloned human cells revealed how perception controls behavior and gene activity. Lipton's current research on the biochemical pathways connecting the mind and body provide insight into the molecular basis of consciousness. For more information about Bruce Lipton, Ph.D., and his work, check his web site: **www.brucelipton.com**

Nancy Marie is a gifted intuitive, author and illustrator who has taught intuitive development for the last 25 years. Ms. Marie is known internationally for her highly accurate readings and her innovative teaching techniques using breath, sound and movement. She is an enthusiastic and interactive speaker with a talent for explaining even the most esoteric subjects in such a way that any-one, whether on a spiritual path or not, can grasp their meaning.

In 1997 Nancy wrote and illustrated her first book, *The Beckoning Song of Your Soul: A Guidebook for Developing Your Intuition* (ISBN 0-9660418-0-1). For more information about Nancy Marie or her current speaking schedule, check her web site: **www.innereyepublishing.com**